Isolation

A Timeless Account

Ilene Terry Polinsky

Copyright © 2021 Ilene Terry Polinsky

Dedication

I would like to dedicate this book to my mentor, John Burgos. I've observed John grow as an empath, fearless in his life: holding us to a standard that each can gain the sovereignty needed for inner growth. It has been his belief in my ability to rise up as the "solo act" I've always been, which sustained me through a maddening isolation. This book emanated from that support. Thank you, John Burgos!

Forward

    This book serves as an account of my experience with isolation, as would a diary. It is almost a daily journal of my repeated feelings, thoughts, and fears for fourteen months. My friend Tom did not relate, for he did not isolate, except when he had Covid. This book will not speak to everyone, and it is not really written for that purpose. Well, I do not really know who will pick up this book, and say "Yes, I too get you!" It is a time in history unlike any other, and so is this experience with a pandemic, and socio-political upheaval.

    My story is one person's interpretation of what 14 months of silence feels like. I found that writing music, and now this book became my solace. I was my own support system, and even hugged myself when I opened my eyes each morning to find that "Yes, we really are here alone."

    I am a living "testimonial" to the power of music, and how that alone can transform, as well as transport one's spirit to a place of love and support. My guides were there every step of the way in the process. In fact: they have not really left my side, as I re-assimilate, and reintegrate back to a semblance of this "new normal."

Isloation: A Timeless Account

Just as in Do Re Mi let's start at the very beginning. What is available to each of us, is where we designate the beginning to be. Since the last year has changed everything about who we are and how we live: let us start there. I am past that "certain age", and so life became an imposed isolation. I found what would support this internal time, and that was writing. Part one of the isolation was about shoring up the music that was in my heart to write. Now that the "door" has started to open, offering a way out, I have turned to writing the "where's the book?" book.

  I have known for at least five years that those pesky guides, and teachers I have been surrounded by, have more than suggested I write a book that will open eyes, and change lives. Some guides are in human form, as this one. Hans would ask me in many mini sessions: "Spirit would like to know: Where's the book?" So, I am now hearing a collective sigh of relief as I endeavor to begin this tome.

  Every day when I awaken, I try to remember where I just was, in a dream. Then I ask myself about this "new reality" and again find that this is not also a poorly constructed dream. I am not excited to learn that this day is like the day before, and that the world is no longer a place where I feel safe and supported. What I also have learned, over the course of the past year, is what I am internally constructing that *is* safe, and supported.

It has become a time of "do it yourself" where there is an exploration of all the things people once did for you, that you now are compelled to do for yourself. Why? Because isolating dictates that. So, I have taken the year to not only write, but also to be creative with all I need to live in a world of my own design.

What is Perspective?

What does it mean to see things from this quiet, protected environment? I am grateful for the opportunity to own my thoughts, creations, and choices. From the moment I open the door just to purge the garbage into the 4th floor "room" where everyone separates each category of "garbage," my world becomes a less safe place. And when I go down to the lobby, or venture out to the actual "outside," there is a level of trust that simply is not the same. The world smells, sounds, and looks like we have arrived at a planet other than Earth. And when I choose to listen to those who have been put in charge of the United States, there is a level of shock at how civilization has become utter turmoil.

I feel a lot like a balloon on a windy day. It gets blown from one end of the spectrum to the other, with no clear trajectory. I know that I must be as internal as I can and ground myself often through the day. Each day becomes another challenge, feeling like the Universe is testing me to immerse in activities that keep the balance, and where love can be an integral part of the mix. I know that I have made it this far, and there is just a short sprint left until the "finish line".

Finish Line

That "finish line" is now in sight! I have crossed that first "hurdle" with vaccine part one! Vaccine part two will open the windows and doors to a freedom of my own making. For no one knows what the new normal looks like yet. This "learning curve" is something all of us are creating together. So, there is a target date of April 1st when I will be served my "walking papers" and safely tread the earth! What a great place to start another level of my evolution!

Perspective on Leadership

It has been a year of uncertainty, with the pandemic, and with leadership in Washington feeding the world with falsehoods and ignoring the needs of the collective. There is language, and communication that simply does not have truth attached. I have seen a large portion of the country (and world) affected by outcomes they did not create, in this frightening, dysfunctional reality! Many have left the planet: more than all wars combined, and it is not over yet. It is a massive shift that many have decided to leave for higher realms.

Choice

There is another thing to ponder: choice. I think about that a lot. We are here on this earth with the power to choose how our lives "play out." I had a good deal of time to explore this during my isolation. What about all those people who were becoming sick with Covid-19, and then either recovering, or leaving their bodies? Did they come here this time, with that choice written in their "contract?" Yes, it was, and yes, they did. We all know when we incarnate, what the "agreements" are. It is astounding how many have left from the "virus," and some left for other reasons! And it all leads back to wondering: "Did I really choose to be here?" "Of course, you chose to be here" (says one of my guides.) It feels like a carousel that just keeps going round and round.

      The numbers go up, the numbers go down. Some days the people seemingly making decisions for the world agree. And there are days that those same elected officials cannot agree on anything. I am quite perplexed at all that we do not know about this "virus." Will we ever know its origin, and whether it is really a virus at all?

Purging

      Retrospectively, we must go backwards to go forward: that is the value of seeing from retrospect. I have seen over a month of the "good guys" leading the United States to feel a bit more hopeful and grounded. Perfect timing with the vaccine part two in a couple of weeks. We see a collective with much to do, as well as me looking for inner guidance to decide what I want to do with "cleaning up my house" figuratively and physically. There is a lot of purging to do with a year of isolation.

It is easy to collect dust, papers, and useless items which seem to fall "under the radar" which causes a huge mess. I will enlist help from those who are deemed safe to come into my abode. It is the perfect time for me to question whether this sanctuary still meets my needs. Maybe it is a time of purging more than things. It goes deeper, and perhaps it is time to purge the sanctuary. After all, it is just an enclosure that supported me for a year or more of isolation, and too many years of growth from performer to teacher, to writer/composer, to playwright. Maybe it is time for these "walls" to come down, and others to replace them! Perhaps Long Beach really awaits!

What is so ironic is how I have let go of family who have been a source of a big disturbance to my inner peace. And one who is part of a childhood extended family, has returned after searching for me for a while. He misspelled my name, and hence could not find me until this pivotal point with the pandemic. What I have repeatedly learned is that there aren't any coincidences. Everything happens at the precise time, with all the players in place.

Time and Distance

Is it Friday again? It is as if the calendar is playing with my mind. Despite the isolation, time is moving faster than before. Perhaps it is the anticipatory time before the vaccination completion when I can move into that space of unknown newness and create what is my day to day "normal." We have two weeks of discovery before we can do that process. So, let us enjoy the ride!

Counting the days until "vaccine day," my body is already anticipating and finding this period hard to digest. It is flat out uncomfortable. My friends are really helping me a lot to release the stress. It is the home stretch after an entire year of learning a new way to function in this unrecognizable world. The masks alone create distance. Couple that with social distancing and there is no meaningful exchange, except on one of the video chats online. Zoom is a smashing success, and has become, in some ways, a lifeline for many.

Vaccinated or not, people are still feeling tentative about what is safe. The "rules" keep changing as the world finds out more about this "uninvited guest."
I am done with my post vaccine "blues" (sounds like a hit song!) There are 11 days left for this isolation! So, I am finishing my experience with this year. All that needs to be said/felt/done, will happen in the next 11 days. Then the road is paved for a new experience with this "new normal."

The World Changed

The songs that were written for this time in isolation pale compared to "What Now?" for this song clearly has a "split personality." Half was written before we all were told to shelter in place, The other half was written when the confusion was so clearly resounding the question: "What just happened?" Each time I sing this song, I hear the "before and after" and feel two quite different things. I cry as I sing the last half. It is so confounding how we were led to this place where the entire world changed.

We are still not sure what that change will be--- for many countries, as well as states are still surging in numbers. It seems a simple command: "wear your mask." Some are still not convinced, for the former leader of the US confused many with his opposition to this command. His indignance, and insanity will be remembered in the history books as what may have caused more of a calamity than necessary. He turned his back on the pandemic, as the infection/death numbers rose astronomically.

Crowning and Release from Captivity

There must be some symbolism with a broken tooth, because as I count down the days to my release from this asylum, I also count the days until my tooth can begin to be healed and "crowned." So, for the purpose of keeping some sort of levity about it all, I will leave on the 31st to begin my ceremonial release, and "crowning ceremony" simultaneously. Perhaps I need to order a mask that contains a picture of a Queen with her headdress, or just settle for a pre-release ceremony. After all, it has been a "one woman show" until now!

It is the weekend before the official release from captivity, and the sky was a beautiful backdrop for me to begin the celebration. I spent my usual 5-10 minutes outside, before returning to my protected environment. The Spring weather has been just sparkling and the trees are awakening from a challenging winter. Spending so much time inside has been painful and confusing for me. Time and timing are not what they once were. I have learned all too well what "being in the moment" really means.

Tomorrow's full moon has around eight planets "holding hands" with each other, as the energy is beautifully potent. Dreams are also confusing, as I awaken wondering where the "reality" is. The question is: "What moment are we present in?" Perhaps this release from the isolation will provide more grounding into the present. We will know in four days. That is such a welcome thought!

Such a plethora of mixed feelings about this release from my protected enclosure. Some call it a cage or pen for animals. This was not the same, for I was not from the "wild." Yet the release feels strangely like an animal being released. My back really has been in knots since this is so much about venturing out into a future that does not contain what I knew from before. There was plenty of time to create masterpieces from my creative mind. What cannot be created is the future.

What isolation taught everyone is how much we can only be in the present. That is, after all, the only thing that we can create in. So, the beautiful music, and this book will follow me as I find myself and many who I could not visit. Such bittersweet reunions with family, friends, and new friends that "happened by" on the Facebook groups I was part of. What a shift from the ability to only hug myself for over 13 months! Such is what we will call "Sunday before."

I had so much to do with the tooth issue, that I was in that energy a bit earlier than expected. So, part one of restoration of a particularly important tooth began the day before the "fanfare." And what a lengthy restoration that was. The office was in the financial district where people likely to be Trump connected were numerous, recognized without masks. I prayed and knew that I was protected by my friendly guides, and I let go of the fear.

Fanfare, and Release

Today's "fanfare" was subtle. Part one was returning to my beloved health food store. It was weird, yet very recognizable. I did not see the entire "family" for I arrived early. I made the decision to return every 3 or 4 days. It is as if the 13 months began to melt into oblivion today! This afternoon, I will visit my local Chiropractor, and begin to feel that my body is moving toward health. He is also like family…he has been in my life for at least 10 years. This reunion was very welcome.

As is the case with most things of great importance, I am still in the transition phase. So many things were changed to suit a time of being in a cocoon, that most animals in a cocoon do not just hop out. There is an audition for the "greater stage," and then all species "fly the coop." I have been on two excursions, had a very strange night with a "screaming computer," and am in a kind of limbo with something else that was planned for today.

So tomorrow might be the selected day to take me "over the top" into that new world that will remain nameless. For this is the time for moving through the uncharted territory with the curiosity of a child. And we will stay in this exploration for a bit more, to put a "ribbon" on it.

Discovery: What Happened to Bill?

Today was another day of exploration of this amazing neighborhood. I walked home again from PT, to get more of my body back and to see, feel and sense the way everyone has changed. I do not need to know these people at all to feel that some "get it" with what each is asked to do for the collective to be safer and healthier than they have been in over a year. So, I passed by those who just would not comply with the simple "rule of thumb:" wear a mask! I walked around as many as I could and left the rest to the forces that are there to protect.

I then met a neighbor I had not seen in over a year. She is still mourning the death of her husband. He was one of the first to contract the Covid virus. It was so new; she was able to be with him until he passed. The doctors thought he had cancer, when in fact, it was Covid. Now that I am out of my sanctuary, I am discovering people I have known for decades--and the changes are astounding!

The In between

I have learned in record time that there is no smooth transition from isolation to emancipation. It is three days into post-vaccine freedom, and I find myself in "the in between." My legs are not familiar with the walking I once did each day. I took two long walks in the past three days, and my legs are very sore.
My advice to self: "go easy." There is no way to erase fourteen months of stasis, and reduced mobility, and get "back in the saddle". It is now the "in between" until I feel the same energy I once had. Patience, Ilene!!

Catching Up With Crucial Exams

And patience was needed when I visited doctors for exams that were postponed until after the vaccination. Two very excruciating and lengthy exams were performed. In the best of times, they caused a fright that is difficult to describe. This time, the waiting between the exams, in an indoor environment, was truly uncomfortable.

Then, to find out that the rules changed with the pandemic. No longer did we get the test results the same day, through the radiologist. The choice was to panic, as I did the last time, or simply wait, and go to sleep. I chose the latter, after trying to decipher images already posted, and THEN I panicked! So, there was a third person, who comforted me, and gently asked me to go to sleep. The next morning, a letter was in my file from the radiologist, congratulating me on a normal test result. I am sure I will frame the letter.

Physical Therapy: One road to recovery

Yesterday was the exact opposite of the day before. I had a face- to- face physical therapy session. My body woke up in a way that I had not felt in 14 months. It was amazing to have someone touch my back, and legs, and help me move them again! Virtual physical therapy just did not work! And to be in a large facility with others working out was exhilarating! It was like coming out of a long, deep sleep! Then walking into a pharmacy and picking up a prescription for the first time in the same 14 months was so simple, and amazing. No more apartment building volunteers to help! They were wonderful, but I needed that experience of going back into the pharmacy again, and reconnecting.

Reconnections, or Maybe Not

Today was about reconnecting with my "family" at the hardware store. The manager and I have known each other for more than 20 years. He was so worried about what happened to me: it was very emotional, and so sweet! All these experiences are a way to "get my feet wet" again and find that "new normal" with the mask covering my face.

What is an unfortunate byproduct of isolation, are the ones that we have been forming "friendships" with: supporting as we all hold on. However, as we begin to move through the in-between, we may find that those "friendships" are quickly disappearing. And it's okay: it's a sign of progress as the finish line approaches.

My guides are very protective and honest, and sometimes show me that a lot of isolation was fantasy. Or at least it was showing a world changing into something else. Until I walked out into that new normal, I had no idea what might be found. Perhaps friends awaiting my return to the outside, and 20-year friendships continue in whatever way they are now.

What's Next?

Part of me is resisting that next step. It is exhausting, confusing and provocative. Whether people out there who resist wearing a mask, or the impatience I feel with how walking causes so much exhaustion. There are decisions that need to be made on all those "next steps" with transportation, appointments missed for a year, or who remains from the pool of people I met in that Zoom fantasy. It isn't smooth, and it isn't progressing at a pace that's comfortable. It's slow, methodical, and needs to unfold "out there" and in its own time.

I am quite clear about balance. I finished working with physical therapy, after a difficult night, and yet I felt the need to walk. See the neighborhood again: admire the cherry blossoms, and all the trees that just woke up the past couple of weeks. I did the almost mile walk home, and it was exhilarating! It took me past that threshold of exhaustion, but it didn't matter. It was the walk of finding beauty, and reacquaintance with what once was 15 months ago.

It still is not clear what life will continue to be, as I walk that same path in a different way. Seeing so many familiar faces, cut off by a mask (at least those who agree to wear one.) Recognition is reduced, and old friends are not always greeted, for they too don't see me. This new normal is certainly a challenge, and one that changes as more is known about this virus, and how it impacts all of us, even those of us who have vaccinated. It is an example of how we always lived with things that were not known. That crescendo has grown. It is our obligation to ourselves to continue to live in the confines of what we create, not what is dictated to us by the country's leaders.

What Now?

Today is a sad day for me. I have had days like this, when I think of the song, I wrote half-in and half-out with the pandemic ("What Now?") The first half was innocent, with hope that we would somehow "figure this thing out," and the second half was written when I knew that the world would never be the same again. I sing it, as I did today, and the meter of the song does not match the accompaniment.

It is a way of saying that anything from that time was energetically a different flow: contrasting with what it is now. Part of me wants to go back, but most of me knows that it is not possible for the earth to withstand the old energy where it is now. And it is not just the pandemic: it is the people: they cannot seem to acknowledge that we are all connected. The government is one big mess.

They cannot even agree that the "Insurrection" on January 6th was the worst attack on our government (and that includes the two World Wars). There is destruction between groups of people: religious upheavals, racial upheavals involving law enforcement, and mass shootings. The government will not agree that maybe there is some way to restrict these "killing machines." I know that Gaia is impatient, and awaits an answer to Her question: "can you work this out amongst yourselves so that I can continue to exist?"

The Birds

I went out today to listen to the birds again. It was just after a period of rain, so the birds were not singing much. Instead, I spoke to a neighbor I had not seen for many months. It is remarkable how different the expression when half your face is covered, especially your mouth. As a singer, I understand the muted sound of a covered mouth.

This "in-between" is exhausting. My body became accustomed to a much slower pace, and it was a rhythm that helped me to become introspective. That introspection allowed a great deal of inner growth. When the isolation was officially over for me, the rhythm outside of the confines of my apartment was more than my body could tolerate. It is a gradual process that requires patience, and sleep when it is needed.

The birds are confounding me. There is more than one species, in various locations. They all have different interpretations of the earth's flow. So, I will have to choose one, and record the "song" they are singing. That will provide the layer of sound for me to create an accompaniment. It is a "first" for me, and so it has no presumed outcome. But then, this time is all about being free of outcomes. When I go to sleep, I ask my guides to please help me remember the "other story" going on in my sleep. It seems to be all about another group of people that I know and have a different life with.

Masks or Not?

Today's walk was a bit confusing. The rules changed again, and people were told: if you vaccinated, you do not need the mask outside. In some cities, that may be okay to tell people. But I am in NYC, and there are many who did not wear masks before. They are doing the same now. They are opposed to getting vaccinated, and this could prolong the "herd immunity" they are all waiting for. It has been a guessing game since the beginning with who may have the virus and who is asymptomatic. There are laws protecting everyone's right to govern their own bodies, so the guessing game continues.

Birds and A New Vibration

I am beginning to study the sounds of the various bird species. There is a rhythm that adds a counterpoint that blends well. My next song may be all about the birds, and their new sounds and rhythms. Every species, including humans are adhering to Gaia's new movement that provides the musical meter. It is fascinating! It seems that there is no carryover from what we experienced pre-pandemic. I feel, deep down, that this change is all positive.

When the pandemic was at its peak, the president and Washington turned a deaf ear to a world that was releasing people to the "other side" at warp speed. We all had no choice, but to wait until the election was over. The new administration would handle this scourge in a much more humane way. It was a time of holding one's breath and staying close to home. Thank goodness, NYC was improving with many following mask and cleanliness protocols.

I will use the birds to represent how the flow has changed and write a piece for the birds. That piece will end with what the resonance has become to this point. I know that it is a fluid movement that will continue. As we are introduced to new people, I have introduced us to a new flow.

It is a pleasant Spring Day, and I will continue the "research" on the birds. It is a perfect metaphor for change: examine the sound and rhythm of the birds. Since I never did that before, there is an acceptance that the rhythm and sound has changed. The only proof of this "pudding" is how the rhythm of my music has changed. So, the experiment makes sense to continue.

Purging at the East River

Another welcome reacquaintance was with the Divine Mother in the form of the East River, and the Promenade that is adjacent to the water. It is where I have always come to purge whatever needs to be released. The past 15 months would be a prime example of a "motherload" of purging. I stood in front of the river, with the backdrop of the skyline of New York City, and prayed as I purged. It added another quarter mile to my walk home, but it was well worth it. It most definitely was on the list of the "In Between" to complete.

I have become rather uncomfortable with planning: what I plan to do for any given day, can become something else. That has always been the case, just not with the frequency since the isolation began. Weekends have always been a challenge for me. Part of it is remembering those Sundays with my brother at that horrible facility. He had a good time with us, but I could feel the isolation he felt when we were preparing to leave. Suffice it to say: Sundays have an energy all their own, as each one included my brother, and how I remember 1955, as if it were yesterday. What is good about this time coming out of isolation, is they are all here to support me through each step leading out of my sanctuary.

Mother's Day

Mother's Day was somewhat melancholy, despite Mom being in the ethers. She has been there since the pandemic started. I sang the song Mom always referred to as Daddy's song. He never heard it for it was written after he left his body. However, the cabaret show that I did in his memory, included the song that was dedicated to him ("The Wind Beneath my Wings.") It is a song describing someone with selfless love for another. Dad really had that kind of love for me. So, a short walk, and a feeling of connection to Mom was enough.
Somehow, this book is being written to help Gaia through this energetically unstable time. What is rock solid is this book! The bird song will have to wait a bit.

The Facelift

Okay, let's move! Today could be considered a bridge that swings one into moving out figuratively, or physically. The apartment is finally getting a "facelift" by the management. The bathroom has been an "eyesore" for the entire year, with stubborn mold that has cost many nights of sleep. One must breathe clean air, and that was not an option until now. The workers have been vaccinated, as have I, and away we go, into (or back to) the unknown. The energy that has been slow to catch up, is doing just that, starting today! It is just after the New Moon, and I have an arm's length of things I want to do again, as I continue to discover the "new normal."

The smell exuding from the cleaning solvent is not pleasant, but acceptance is the key here, as the smell leads to removal of a dangerous mold.

My Friend who Made it Through Covid

In the middle of this commotion, was a visit from my friend Tom. This is our first visit since the lockdown 15 months ago. Tom was at "death's door" with Covid 19 and was able to direct energy to his lungs to raise the level of oxygen to keep from being intubated. Quite a strong will to heal the body! And he did, along with around 200 of us "holding space" for him. But he did it and is also vaccinated. So, today, with all the vaccinated workers doing various things, and my friend, this apartment was crowded! I learned a valuable lesson about healing the body. Some of it is physical but most is about love. Love heals more than anything else could! And it is! Some days carry small steps, and some giant leaps. This one was huge!

Mask Confusion

Just at the point of understanding the rules with masks, the CDC changed their minds! Everyone is confused and has been since life took a turn. Those who have been vaccinated now are told they can shed the masks both inside and outside. They also do not need to socially distance. There is so much confusion, especially the question about those who did not vaccinate, and who may be asymptomatic, or symptomatic.

To the layperson, there is a bit of apprehension about this guidance. We continue to walk shoulder to shoulder with the big question about who is walking next to me? I am feeling, once again, confusion about these rules that don't seem to make sense. This is one of those times, when I will decide based on that inner voice that knows best. It has been one big experiment since we learned about this virus.

The CDC claims they have been working on vaccines for this type of virus for quite a few years. However, the CDC is only one aspect of what we are each learning about how to behave in this new normal, which seems to be changing about as rapidly as the information we are receiving.

Melancholy Sunday

Call it a setback, or another Sunday, but tonight is melancholy and feels like the missing pieces of my life are still missing. Immediate family has "flown the coop," and there is not much to be done with that. There are not many knocks on my door, and it is still that lonely place it was for 14 months. Reversals of this magnitude don't just mysteriously happen. Time is the best healer, and this type of isolation doesn't just end. So, whether we are still in the in-between, or fully present, is a matter of perspective. I simply am not grounded in any one place yet, and I guess that's normal in this anything but normal time.

My guides have not been terribly vocal lately, and that has added to the loneliness. All that I had, is all I have now: her expression. Whether through music or this book, it has been my lifeline. And the lingering question remains: why do I write my best when I feel my worst? Such a tender time, and a good time to remember what all who remain important to me say: "You're never really alone," and, "Your vulnerability is your strength."

Timelessness

As I literally bounce from in-between to present and even back to isolation, the message from Gaia is "time is no longer linear." That is one of the great shifts that happened alongside the other changes, especially all the countries, states, and cities shutting down. During that process came the "great shift" to a different clock.

Mundane Has its Perks

Each day is an adventure, and it can either flow, or get a little stuck. Today began with me finally feeling that it was safe to do something as mundane as the wash downstairs. It was awkward, and strange, with sanitizer and alcohol as "chasers" for the act of doing one's wash. But it was done quickly, and part two will be in a couple of days.

I will minimize the hand wash, as it really does not clean well, and the drain gets stopped up with fabric. I asked a favor of management, and they cleared the drain so that I do not have to deal with the other manager who is quite difficult. Day by day the apartment gets more of a "facelift," and the pleasure of the mundane is indescribable! But then, nothing is mundane: it is all in the interpretation!

My Once Family

Every so often, I am reminded that my family is thriving on another level of existence. I took a "stroll" through Facebook and noticed them celebrating a huge milestone for my grandniece. No one stepped forward to share the news. I looked at the screen with the least amount of connection I can remember. There was no "why didn't you tell me?" or tears of feeling excluded. I did write a congratulatory post and was thanked.

That is probably the last revisit for a good while, and it is okay. It is as if they were climbing a mountain, light years away, and the peak seemed to be like a star off in the distance: not close enough to establish communication. Is it sad? I do not really know the entire "story" yet. Coming out of isolation reminded me that I let go of so many things/people/attachments! It unfolds to me at its own pace. It is an invitation for me to step up to this new vibration, without feeling that I have any power to take anyone else on this solo journey.

Freedom in This Timelessness

The story keeps unfolding to you, the reader, and I, one who sits and waits for the story to continue. Each day leads to the next, with little expectation, except a general outline of chores, etc. Last night, as I was walking home from PT, I decided to take my mask off, as suggested by the CDC, and there was a sigh of relief as I freed myself from this object of separation. It was peaceful, and I felt a closer connection with all the people I passed along the way home. Some looked at me questioningly, and some just smiled.

It is such a huge time of change: I can feel the confusion from some who cannot decide what to believe about the transmission of this virus.
We are still in the in-between. What I am discovering is this timelessness has almost deleted the sections of this tome. I guess it may change, once again, and perhaps take on the timeless quality it has adopted. With no effort at all, it already has!
The writing of three songs, and this book, is what has kept me in my body. It was the

grounding force that kept my purpose alive, and my heart feeling my love, and the love emanating from the music.

This book is now in the timelessness it was destined for. One question that has resonated in my mind is: "Am I really supposed to be here?" along with "Why am I here?" It gnaws at my very being often. Yesterday, my guides finally answered me with this: "This is the life you chose."

Collateral Damages

Isolating was not a choice: it was a life-protective decision. As the isolation passed the one-year point, my body began to show signs of damage, for it was a time of little movement, and not enough sun and fresh air. Those who have vaccinated, and re-entered a different world, life was not simple, or simply "oh let's just continue where we left off."

It was about assessing what happened to "a body in wait" and what happened to a "mind that once responded to linear time." The mind was no longer thinking in a linear way: it was functioning in the moment, and no longer in the past or future. Well, that was the good part: for we can only create in the moment anyway. But my body was literally "sitting around in wait." Even doing PT as I diligently did in "virtual land," was not the same.

What I discovered was a body that was experiencing joint pain, and deterioration, mouth issues with broken teeth, and gum issues. Wearing masks causes one to curtail consumption of water, and lack of oxygen to the facial area. This can cause dehydration, and issues with the areas covered by the masking. Again, it was "survival mode," and I knew no other choice but to follow guidelines and find masks that allowed for more breathing.

Now that we have a respite that is in effect, there will be less need for masking. However, as with isolation, the virus still exists on other parts of the planet. Until the entire planet achieves "herd immunity," the issue is not closed. What I have decided is to be in this moment of levity and enjoy it. Once the body is healed a bit more, a visit to cousins, and to the beach can be considered.

Yesterday's walk home was about how best to "fight the elements" without the proper gear. Somehow, the "weather Gods" were with me, and I managed to walk home unscathed, except for the intense PT that almost landed me on my "keister." Somehow it did not feel like overkill, but just waking up sleepy skeletal areas, muscles, etc. and finding the proper way to feel okay anyway. This time is about the do it anyway, say it anyway, write it anyway, play it anyway, and perhaps do not say it anyway: give it to one of your guides to do it for you! Pretty crafty, and oh so appropriate for those moments that can be averted.

Memorial Day With a Twist

Memorial Day weekend was so sad. The rain described the cold, sad trip outside. It had its moments, but it was mostly quiet, rainy, and low energy. The "high point" for me was a visit to the local pharmacy. It was my first trip to shop for goods I reserved for Amazon. There were bargains for the taking! Such a simple process, but it was the first since last February. The cashier was such a wonderful young man! He explained that the laundry detergent I was about to buy was the same price for three of them. He went upstairs and brought down two others.

There was a sweet exchange, and he even put the bag into my shopping cart, as well as opened the door for me to leave. I thanked him and called him an Angel. He smiled. The class I attended later that day helped to explain this month that includes many "retrogrades" and lots of challenging astrological transits, including the Summer

Solstice. It was the perfect end to an otherwise challenging day.

The Rebound

How does one explain the metaphor of the "double edged sword?" After I finished PT, and walked to and from the facility, I arrived home sore, and felt my heart racing. It was decided among myself and my guides, that perhaps I went far over the threshold of what I was ready for. I went to sleep thinking: "okay: if I awaken in the morning, I'll have another day to complete this work. If not, on some level it will be done."

Yesterday I awakened with the same racing heart as the night before. I decided to call the doctor and was told to come in to have it checked. In the interim of the call and the appointment, there was time to ask my extraordinary empaths on Facebook to assist. Many did. One reminded me of the importance of whether that racing heart was mine, or I was picking up on someone else's energy. What I felt, after the test proved to be fine, is it may be from another dimension, or galaxy other than Earth.

The important element here is release. When there is something disturbing the peace for anyone, release it…and maybe in the releasing, will be the answer. It is not always apparent, or even necessary. We move forward knowing that all is good, and perhaps take it a bit easier the next time. After all: one cannot erase 14 months of captivity in a month or two.

Bird Sense

I heard someone mention on the news that he was listening to a species of birds "speaking" to him. It is comforting to know that others are noticing the communication coming from birds. They are closely "hearing" the sounds of Gaia in her "altered language." Many are feeling a rebound, as I am. When 14 months of emotions left unexpressed gets jarred to the surface, it becomes subject to triggers that will release unexpectedly. The important thing is to work on the body physically to allow for the release to be a positive one, and an outlet for the emotions.

I have not given up on the bird song: perhaps it needs to percolate some more. Finding a quiet time to just hear the birds is difficult in downtown Brooklyn. If it isn't the sound of cars passing by, it's people conversing, or trucks fixing streets. What is needed is a quiet weekday at the beach. Coming up soon!!

Why Them?

In the meantime, I am still exploring: "why them?" Especially the day before my sister's birthday. It will be noticed, but not used as a pathway to reconnection. I tried reaching out last year and the gift card was not touched. I canceled it and used it as a gift for someone else. Gratitude is an elusive word. If not initiated correctly, it becomes a gesture requiring the recipient to notice its pure intention.

Free to Go: Where?

This time is still one that causes the body to react to stimuli in ways that are jarring and fear inducing. Now that we who have been vaccinated are "free to go," there is an abundance of air and sun to soak up, to release the stale air that may still be hovering inside the body and the abode.

Masking and Gums

This week, I get a "gum lift!" It consists of surgery to release infection. Masking can be toxic. Using a mask for long periods of time, causes one to lose sight of water intake. The more that masking is done, the worse it is for the nose and mouth. There is a lack of oxygen to the mouth and gums, triggering infection.

Implications and Innuendos During Retrogrades

Today is a day of huge change: probably precipitated by sis's birthday, and an awkwardly interpreted channeled piece. I shared it with my Facebook group, and got a bit too close to its message, and the lack of response. I took the post down, and another was inserted in its place, with implications and innuendos about how the class has changed, and perhaps has triggered another ending. It is something in process for me, and I will "discuss" this with my guides. Impulsive behavior during all the retrogrades is not wise.

Undoing Damages

We have arrived at the day of undoing the damages to my gums. I went to the health food store this morning to get a sense of what could be consumed while the gums are healing. It's a guessing game, but the supplies are needed to have a start point. Again, the collateral damages are showing up, and are being addressed in order of importance. I will ask the dentist if he has seen or spoken about this anomaly with his colleagues. It seems obvious that many have experienced various mouth and teeth/gum issues at this point. Time to get ready. To be continued...

The surgery was excruciating! Seemed to mirror the emotional toll the isolation has caused. If we were to do a study, there would be many, like me, choosing to clear the passages leading to the mouth, and the expression that was down to a bare minimum for far too long.

March 20, 2020 Triggered a Clock Change

As I assess the "collateral damage" to my mouth and gums, I decided to sing "What Now?" once again. With gums hurting, and body exhausted from a difficult night, I sang that song, and was transported to March 20, 2020. That is the day NYC shut down as the pandemic was dictated by the governor for what to do. All the feelings simply flooded back to that day, and that song, that was already in process. Today, once again, the rhythm of the song, and my "internal clock" did not match. So, I kept stopping, and listening to the rhythm of March 20-28th, when the song was completed. As I repeat the song, I find a tear or two rolling down my cheek, and a song that has its own clock. For it started with hope and ended with a shocking revelation.

The mouth and gums missed the sun so much, that they started to swell, and rebel. Sun coming in through a window is far different than a sun that you feel directly on your skin. And the months passed with little time for visits "outside" and the collateral damage started to accumulate.

Tomorrow is the emancipation of the gums! Sutures come out, and I can eat again. I am sure that I lost 5 pounds more this week from not eating much. Sutures in one's mouth will certainly be cause for eating next to nothing. Thank goodness, there are nutritious liquid drinks!

I promised myself that once the "collateral damages" have been addressed, there is a celebration in my future...like a trip to the beach! Long Beach has waited a looong time for my return. Like maybe 3 years? There are bodies of water that just stand out in their beauty: Long Beach is one of them. We have a date set up for late June.

Emancipated, Yet Tentative

My teeth have been emancipated from a four- month process! It transferred to me, feeling the freedom from total isolation for the first time! Until my teeth were released from all restrictions, I did not feel complete. It is equivalent to nursing a baby back to health. There are very tender areas that need healing time when I can begin to chew normally. What a miracle!

It is just love

If anyone is looking for that "potion" that will "right the ship," it is quite simple: LOVE!
I have been reconnecting with neighbors I have not seen throughout the isolation, and here they all are (at least the ones that did not move somewhere else!)

One neighbor who suffered a loss, has been available (at least until they move next week.) There are so many memories attached to that family, including teaching music to the children two decades ago. In this moment (which is all we have anyway,) it is exhilarating to speak to them, and share both the love and the loss.

Our visits will hopefully continue until they leave next week. My hope is that we will stay in touch, and perhaps visit occasionally. Again, what is present is all we have. The future "is ours to see" (Que Sera, Sera.) That song is from the 1940's, but Doris Day knew that back then. We are all learning that now, as we come out of our abodes, and meet up once again.

Hug

What happens when one is not hugged for 15 months? A lot! One's heart is not massaged, as the rest of the body is by a masseuse. There is no exchange of love from one to the other. Over the course of time, the heart starts to feel foreign to the body. That is when the heart starts to show signs of illness.

This collateral damage is damaging! I am presently discovering that my heart was okay with the love from my angels and guides, as well as my mother, who was always close to my heart. I am treating it medically just to "cover the bases." My guess is over time I will heal. It is still a time of reconnecting with those who I love. I ask my heart to wait just a bit longer…

A Simple Act of Kindness

As I made my way home from PT, I chose the path that I sometimes take, and I know why I did now. As I passed my health food store on the other side of the street, there was a woman who was struggling to get up from a bench she had been sitting on and resume her way with the walker she uses. She was an African American woman, who was too heavy for me to lift her. So, my instinct was to hold the walker and see if she could then lift herself. She did, and she thanked me for helping her.

An act of kindness does not take any thought at all: it is an act. As I excused myself from her presence, two African American gentlemen walked in my/her direction, and gave me smiles that could make anyone's day, and I would say it made mine! I do not know why so many of us are still confused about our connection to each other. I am Jewish, I am an empath, I am a writer, and I am a resident of this earth, where we are all connected to each other. It seems to be taking a long time for each of us to understand that. An act of kindness takes no forethought, or planning. It is an act of doing for another.

I am learning so deeply what the collateral damage has been to this body that I am encased in. Part of me feels as if I am stronger than before isolating, and another part is impatient with this somewhat endless process, though time is no longer measured the same as before. What feels endless, is only a couple of months.

When I look back at where the country/world was before the pandemic, it was not a healthy place at all. We were collectively choking from smoke/fire, wind, and rain. There was no way out but through a rising vibration that took with it the "shadow" that we are still releasing collectively and personally. Everyone has an opportunity to shift in any way they desire. Some are doing a lot of inner work, as I am. Some are acting out their impulses, doing damage to both themselves and many others.

The Fabric Changed

I live in a high-rise building. I have been here much longer than my "welcome mat" (if it had a brain) ever imagined. There were certain people that made up the fabric of this building's beauty. Most left, either for the suburban lifestyle, or for the "other side." I realize that this city, as most others, has radically changed, as the pandemic affected so many small businesses, and performance venues.

Today became the official day to say "goodbye" to my wonderful neighbors, who vowed they would never leave. But a lot of vows changed, in this case, because husband/dad left his body the day before the "lockdown." I saw the movers as I left to get groceries for a few days. I have spoken to them more than a few times before this, but the "official" goodbye is today.

I received my first official hug from the mother of the family, and it was so bittersweet: we both cried. And I am still crying. We made a vow that we will be in touch. She will be back and forth from the apartment until her daughter is settled into a place in the city. This goodbye hurt deeply, and yet it was the greatest flow of love I have felt since before the pandemic. There is that bittersweet again!

Another Piece of Fabric Changed

One of our beloved doormen is retiring. He has been a friend, a "helping hand," and my "light at the end of the tunnel" as I ventured out after isolating. He was able to transcend the Covid infection and come back to us all having recovered. An experience such as that one, can certainly have one rethink one's plans. In his case, I do not think any of his plans changed, but he held firm on retirement.

Time for Change

As many of us are coming out of isolation, we are rethinking choices that no longer fit. I crave the ocean so much more than before. I want to live there (if I were a mermaid, I would live there.) I want it to be accessible to me: I could always get a keyboard and play on the beach for support (only when it is warm, not hot.) But it is time for a change that requires me to think about how to manifest this change.

I have no attachment to anything material. I have no need to bring anything with me but electronics, and my piano. A few clothes too, for we cannot scare the "neighbors" (that was a joke.) But now that I chose to be here at this time, it is important to share this book, and all the music I have written the past 15 years. It is not about ego either: it is about helping others in the way that music has helped me.

As I write this section, I am now aware that I am coming to the close of this section of the book, and of this chapter of my life. It is time to do due justice to the retrospect. It will reflect the time immediately prior to the pandemic. It will also reflect memorable times in my professional life and childhood.

Then we truly have gone forward to go back, as the book dictated from the beginning. What beginning?

Isolation Part 2: A More Current Perspective On Isolation

Isolation Continues
It is a similar experience, despite the freedom to leave the apartment. I have not visited family or friends since the emancipation.
There is a certain freedom I am grateful for. But there is a tentative feeling about travel. In New York, there is around 30% of the population that remains unvaccinated, along with children under the age of 12. Trains are simply not safe for me. There is too much crime, and people who choose to unmask.

I must listen to guidance, which tells me to wait until the dust settles with Labor Day, and the opening of the schools. In the meantime, I walk a lot, observe the beauty of my neighborhood, and walk to physical therapy. The car service continues to be my travel of choice when I have an appointment in the city. It allows me to stay connected to Manhattan without using the trains.

Retrospective

Which retrospective is being referenced? Hold on: I may get you dizzy on this carousel ride! If we keep with the way this book is structured, we will start this retrospective just prior to the time of emancipation. Why not take another look from where we are now and move back? Coming out of isolation was painful, disorienting, and confusing. My body was confused and unsure of where to begin to assess the damages.

I was exhilarated, yet tentative and unsure of how I would travel through this newness. The information that was generated was constantly changing. I knew that I was not ready for any travel other than car services. It was about choice: which appointment is most important? Since I need my teeth and gums to function optimally to eat, my dentist became the first choice. It was a ten-week process, between "crowning" and gum surgery. It was such a blessing to eat food again and use both sides of my mouth!

As weeks passed, I learned about my body's needs, and what I need to do to have greater function of this body I no longer recognize. I lost fifteen pounds from simply eating soft foods and eating much less. The weight loss was another blessing. It is so much easier to tread the earth with less body weight! And tread I must! It is so liberating to take daily walks, either to get food, or walk to the Promenade! I am even walking back and forth to the physical therapist! If I were to measure distance, I would say on a good week, I walk around 5 miles. Now that is a triumph!

What is troubling is how many businesses I knew for over 30 years closed. That is so sad. I walk through a neighborhood made sparse from the pandemic.
Brooklyn Heights was known for its "mom and pop" shops, and small restaurants/diners. People often remarked at how similar the landscape was to Paris. It is now a landscape with "missing teeth" and spaces waiting to be filled. Quite the analogy!
I look back at those first days of finding out what has changed. For one, people did not communicate the way they once did. There were masks preventing any meaningful conversation, unless there were groups of people who knew each other. All I found myself doing was smiling with my eyes, and

waving at those I knew, or so I thought. Between the landscape and the rhythm/vibration of the earth, there were huge changes in how it felt to tread this new earth. Walking back from PT became a necessity. I was eager to learn what it looked like to view my neighborhood that I had not seen in over a year.

      Car services that brought me to appointments were my bridge to Manhattan. Riding through the streets of Manhattan was both exhilarating and sad. I loved seeing places I once frequented and lamented the ones that no longer were there. The West Village seemed a ghost town with all the closed businesses. I made good use of the huge fares by photographing trees, bridges, the East River, and various famous buildings. It was both fun and emancipating!

As I progress with the physical therapy, I am led closer and closer to being fully emancipated. Riding trains and railroads is next on the agenda both for the beach that awaits, and cousins I have not seen in over a year. The Promenade serves its purpose, but nothing compares to my beloved Long Beach!

      On my way to physical therapy, I stopped at a train station that is on ground level. I had the brilliant idea of loading my new metro card at that station, since I did not have to walk steps to do it. Now I know this is a simple process, but nothing is simple after fifteen months of no subway trips. All that was needed was to shift an old metro card balance to the new one. The attendant said she could not transfer the balance, for hers is not one of the designated stations for this process. She mentioned a station about twenty minutes away, and of course, I am not ready to do that.

I did remember that I never put more than twenty dollars into my balance. Therefore, the choice was to forget the old card and load twenty dollars onto the new one. It is beyond comprehension why she did not suggest that in the first place! Now I am happy as a clam with my new card primed and ready to go! She did inform me that metro cards will soon be phased out, with something else in their place. That is when she lost me! I decided to Google the rest!

Purging a la Promenade

There are all kinds of ways to purge. Mine requires water and beauty. The Promenade here in Brooklyn Heights provides just that! I have lived here long enough to hear Divine Mother say lovingly: "Hello, it's you again!" I pray for whatever it is that needs purging. Today was about the neighbor who has issues with drugs and attitude. I lovingly asked Spirit to purge the connection and clean up the communication. My visit was short, for the day is terribly busy. I would not miss an opportunity on a rather tepid day, to visit.

Purging a la Me

Wherever I am, there I am! Purging can happen right here at the computer, or on the phone with a trusted friend. Recognizing that whatever the feeling, or pain, or sadness, it is all temporary. Today, I send all of that I am feeling-- just love. I even send love to that neighbor who is sad, angry, and addicted. She may not want to receive, but I send it anyway. And I step away from the drama to move forward with my life. That's a good thing! Who needs drama 24/7? No one! So, purge away, Ilene! Let it go and keep on letting it go!

Looking back at Lockdown

I remember how sad I felt, along with questioning how I will get through a very tender, confined time. Would I know what to plan, what to buy, how to receive all the essentials? How would I get by without seeing anyone, and hugging anyone? For how long? Could I even see into the future? What future? Will I have my guides to communicate with? Will I write music about this time? What about the song I am in the middle of? Will I be able to finish it? What about this family that is so fractured? Will they care that I am here alone? Will my friend Tony survive the Covid? Who else is sick in the building? Why don't I hear from or see my neighbor Bill, who I always heard down the hall? Why is it so quiet?

That ended up being the beginning of a 15-month isolation. It taught me a lot about how the future is not the concern. The concern is each day leading to the next. One day at a time. Sometimes it was one moment at a time. Listening to the silence. Listening to my angels and guides that I was able to hear clearly through the silence. The strength I felt was not only mine: it was generated from those inner guides telling me to keep going. It was the music that kept being channeled through. It all defined my purpose and reason for staying.

Looking Back at Relationships

Since everything was changing, so were the people in my life. Some that I knew for a short time, and some that I knew for decades. As I changed with the work I was doing, everyone else was changing too. However, one cannot measure change: it is whatever each decides to commit to. Some relatives were on the cusp of rare or no communication. As time passed, the phone calls became less frequent. I knew that the new friends in my Facebook groups became my family. It was my saving grace along with my guides who kept communicating their support.

As the isolation continued, so too did my friendships grow with this new family, along with my mentor John, who was my guardian angel. One of the long relationships collapsed after a chasm grew between us, on too many beliefs and perspectives in this new normal. I've grown accustomed to this inner work, and I'm no longer afraid of what is to become of this body. And then there is post Covid Tom. He is the same aloof, yet caring individual he was before the pandemic.
If I call him, we talk. If I see him, wetalk.No grand gestures, just talk. If I need something, he usually helps. He is genuinely generous, but not the friend I can hang out with.

My life seems to be partitioned into the teaching, performance, composing, and literary segments. There is another segment, placed purposely in its own category, and that is romance. Since we are timeless in this tome, I will address the romance segment first. Oops, I guess I forgot the family segment: that segment ended with my parent's generation that is now on the "other side."

Back again to the romance segment, which addresses family as well. How is your neck? Did you do a quick turn to the side as I jumped around (or did I?)
My brother, Irving, was the best teacher of what love really is. His body was compromised, and he did not converse as most others do. But he loved so unconditionally, yet not physically. My parents were afraid he would do harm, because of one of the anomalies he was born with. He loved at a distance. I find that very ironic, considering what I was faced with having to isolate for fifteen months, with no one to hug. Guess who was quite present during that entire isolation? He was!

I knew that Irving's unintentional teaching would spill over into my romantic life. And it did. It was a repetition that became so apparent, I could have written the script myself. Whether male or female, the connection, and disconnection was the same. My last romantic connection ended on Valentine's Day, 2006.

When a sibling who demonstrated such enormous love, suddenly leaves his body, the impact can last a lifetime, and it has. After enduring 15 months of an isolation that had no end date, to pick up one's life and start again is not easy when it is preceded by 72 years. I have been assured by my guides that I am still an integral part of this enormous transformation on the planet. I will stay and do what I was intended to do in this life.

Back to Present

We are, after all, timeless! I had two appointments in my beautiful city, sandwiched around my first bus excursion in 17 months. What I will remember is not the two practitioners I saw today, but that liberating experience on the bus. The driver was kind and helpful, and the passengers were distanced perfectly. No one really talked to anyone, but I did not feel any tension either. It was just a pleasant two-mile trip.

Communication

Oh my, how that has changed! I have known, as a teacher, that one size does not fit all. Even twenty years ago, I never considered that each student would learn the same thing in the same way. Sometimes, when I taught a complex lesson, I would do it two days in a row, and not say anything. Most students absorbed it, saying nothing. Some said, "You just taught us that!" I would mutter something like "I know, but it was really important to say it again." Never did I say to any student: "I knew you wouldn't get it the first time," for that would be the highest level of disrespect.

Saying whatever I was teaching with love was key. It is not, after all, basic training: it is a loving, learning environment. Now, as a music healer, I am keenly aware of the importance of attaching love to anything I teach. As I work with different empaths, I look for that same level of respect. When it is not present, the young Ilene tunes out. It happened recently, and she checked out again. It's not personal, or a "knee jerk" reaction, it is just leaving the room where love was not present. In essence, I was being challenged that I was not aware I was feeling the same anger I attracted.

After all, we are each "a work in progress," and we need to honor that possibility in each other. There is so much else to say in this retrospective on teaching, but this is how I am functioning now as a former teacher of music, and a present teacher of music healing.

Christian

This is clearly a time of retrospect for all of us. So much has changed with communication, trust issues, how we will move into the next phase of our time on earth, and so much more. This book is a timeless account of how isolation has affected me as an example of many. The commitment to self, and what is involved in self-care, keeping updated with essentials, and communication with others, has been overwhelmingly difficult.

Many of us are only partly aware of the effect isolation has on the body, mind, and emotional body. What has been helpful for me, is to look at the whole picture, present, past, and how I am building a future. I have a former student who has consistently reminded me of a time when I taught music to thousands of students, over the span of 25 years. It is a distant memory to who I am now, but a relevant one to understand how I got here. And so, there is a departure.

Christian, who I have been in contact with the past five or so years, has agreed to do an interview with me. He will explain how it was back in the 90's with me as his music teacher, and how that has all changed as he has gotten to know the composer/singer/pianist, and writer. He can lend perspective in a way that I may not be able to see.

As we all move forward, there is that link we have to ourselves as the sum of all our experiences, relationships, and growth. At this time of enormous change, it is helpful to look at the sum of all those parts and decide what feels right with the change that our souls are pointing to.

In His Words

I remember the first time I knew I wanted to be in the Steel Band class. It was the first performance by a Steel Band I had ever seen. The music was fun, and the instruments were unique. I was in the 6th grade and had chosen art as my skill class in the performing arts school. Immediately, I regretted not having chosen music. For the rest of that year, I had no choice but to go to art class. I was convinced that the next two years at Alexander Burger, I would be a part of the steel band. That's exactly what I did, thanks to your accepting my request to be in your class.

There is a sixth-grade requirement of xylophone, but you accepted me anyway. I was always grateful to you for that.

The first time I set foot in the classroom, I remember you had all the drums set in perfect order: leads in front, altos behind leads, tenors behind them, and bass/double bass off to each side. In front of the classroom was the piano. You often sampled the music we were learning to play so we knew what it was supposed to sound like. I remember little things, like the smell of the classroom: a smell that emanated from the instruments made from recycled oil drums. It's funny, when I am somewhere and the scent of something like that smell hits me, it makes me think of being in that classroom. Kind of like the smell of popcorn at the movies, or the smell of cotton candy at a carnival. My brain floods with happy thoughts.

I loved having you as my music teacher. You were the first true introduction I had to music. I always heard it on the radio, but never really understood the level of hard work it took to create a piece. You were all business when instructing, and that made me gain such a high level of respect for you. I'm sure it might have been hard to tell from your point of view, but I had a huge admiration and appreciation for you because of your enthusiasm for music. How you, through your example, made us little students want to wrap ourselves in it as well. I would observe closely while you played the piano and would be so impressed with your level of coordination of the keys and pedal.

    You taught us many lessons that had little to do with music. Through all your actions it was easy for me to know that you truly did care about us. I remember the field trips you took us on, and some of the places I visited on those trips. It would be my first and only time going there: like Carnegie Hall. I remember packing our drums into buses and riding out to different places around New York to perform. I felt like a rock star at times, to have been part of such a unique group and getting loud rounds of applause after playing our songs. It was always hard working with you to take those trips and pack all these fragile instruments, but you always did it for us, despite the high level of stress.

    As the years went on and my brain matured, I got to appreciate more and more the experiences I had thanks to you being so wonderful to me. There are some classes I have taken throughout the course of my life that I have completely forgotten about, and some that, for some reason or another, I seem to remember. Your class is one that goes beyond remembering for me. Your class represented for me pure joy, and bliss. No doubt this is the reason why I will always hold you in my heart as being the teacher that had the most impact. It says everything when all these years later, even before we reconnected, my brother and I would still talk about you, and would hope that, wherever you were in the world, you were doing great. We would talk about the songs we played all the time, of course argue about who was better as a Lead. My parents still express their gratitude for all that you allowed us to experience, and for being what they consider to be an amazing teacher and person.

  These experiences enriched my life by introducing me to something that I love: music. Through this inclusion came an improvement to my self-esteem. Feeling like I was being given the opportunity to be a part of the band allowed me to immerse myself into something I truly enjoyed. It was a significant part of what became an amazing childhood in New York City. Understanding that I was an important part of something special enriched my life by giving me more confidence and belief in my abilities. Confidence was an area I struggled with as an adolescent, which is why a lot of these programs are so important to our youth.

All these years later, I am happy to be able to have conversations with a mentor that had such a huge impression on me. I was lucky enough to find you through Facebook, and immediately wrote you a letter expressing an appreciation for you that I couldn't quite express as a kid. Sometimes I think about our conversations and chuckle a bit when I realize that you are still very much a mentor to me, as well as a dear friend. Sometimes I wonder what all those students that you mentored learned and applied in their own lives. Even a small fraction of that would make the world a little better. I thank you for the special love and attention you gave to all of us, and for always being so gracious to kids who were oftentimes difficult to deal with. I am especially thankful for the timeless friendship we have.

Thank you, Christian, for visiting my past with me, so we each can go forward. You were one of many blessings I had in my life who taught me as much about humility, and a different kind of love that professionals must adhere to.

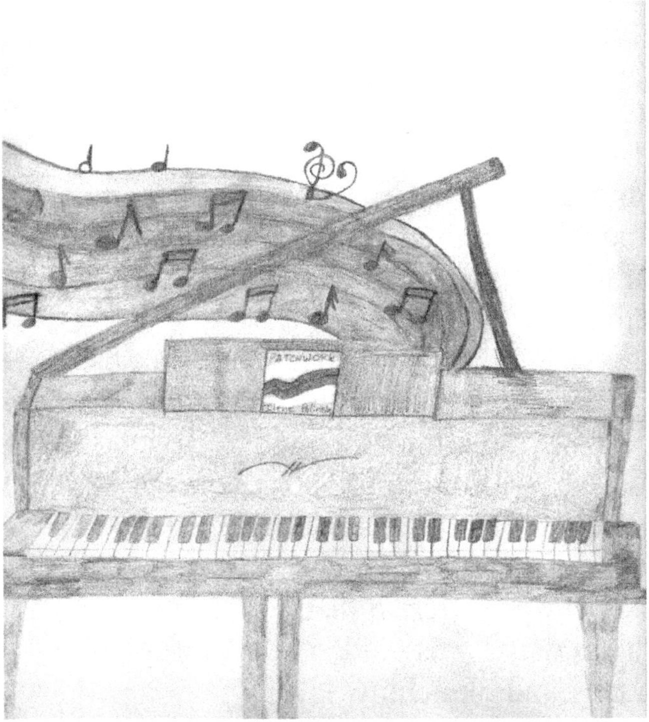
PATCHWORK

Just Love

Continuing where I left off: explaining the absence of love, this is an example of a tender act of love. As I walked to PT, I noticed a young man, clothes disheveled, poking through the garbage for scraps of food. I followed behind, not close enough to give him the three dollars I was instructed by my guides to offer him. He stopped again to rummage through another garbage can and I said loudly: "Excuse me."

He looked up and as I held out the three dollars in front of him, he muttered: "No way!" I said without thought: "God bless you!" He said a loud "Thank you, stay safe." I could tell that he was not homeless long. I guessed that he was recently evicted. His pattern was different than I'd seen before. That's why I was guided to give him the money and bless him.

A simple act that made my day--it was a scripted and timely encounter. I merely followed guidance, and I feel blessed! There is a fine line that divides whether love is present. One can be trained by noted healers who opt to enforce practices rather than lighten up and fill the space with love. The practices will be absorbed either way- but when love is present, there is a deeper lesson.

As I continue my study with renowned healers, I notice my own response to their methods. I could shut off the volume, and not listen to any words, but I will have some type of healing just with the energy coming out of the heart of the healer.

None of the words you are reading are as important as the love that is in every word I write. Every thought I share is not coming from my conscious mind, but rather from my heart. Without that huge love that resides in my heart, I would not have survived the isolation.

The Absence of Physical Touch

It seems the isolation continues despite the trips outside, etc. Why? Because there is still no physical touch. Conversation and seeing friendly faces don't allow this body to respond to a hug, a kiss, or even a pat on the back. Family, whether virtual or genetic, is not present. The pandemic is at a critical point, even here in New York City, where the numbers are good. For me to travel on a train of any kind, is a risk.

There are many who refuse to follow masking mandates, and I have been told of this from those who take the train frequently. Family is a distance from here, and I would have to take a leap of faith to visit. My hope is that something will prompt me to get on that train, despite the risk, knowing I am Divinely protected.

Peeling the Layers

The day is arriving for the apartment to finally be cleaned. Two women will come and assist me in a process that has begun today. Each layer is a memory of the point in isolation where I was entrenched in the work I was doing. The deeper the isolation, the more the layers of dust and papers mounted.

It is astounding how many feelings are returning as I go to another pile of papers and old clothes. Keeping judgment out is difficult. Questions like: why didn't I just throw these things out? Because I was so depressed, lonely, and isolated. I just couldn't focus on meaningful sorting of these things. Knowing that today and tomorrow are just the beginning of this process, lessens the load.

Good or bad, they're now done, and my apartment is a living, breathing space! It's astonishing how much dust accumulates in the strangest places. Kind of how my brain feels at times, as I dust it off for what it has forgotten over the isolation. Is it a product of age, or of this new energy that doesn't remember yesterday, for all that exists is today!

The Rest

When I played flute in the bands in high school and college, I was always engaged in the notes that I didn't play. Why? Because the composer didn't write notes for that group of measures in his/her composition. What did I do during that time? I followed along with the music, and eventually learned everyone else's part, for I was engaged in the process.

Many times, during the pandemic, I sat silent, engaging in the space between what I did that day. I didn't necessarily think or feel anything in that silence, for I disengaged in what may have frightened me in those silences.

Now, as a musician, I still feel those silences. I encourage all of you hearing this book that I am imparting to you: honor those silent moments that I am intentionally inserting for you to know that sometimes there aren't words. Sometimes those rests, or spaces between notes/thoughts, are what we need to visit with our hearts. Don't cut those visits short. Be with yourself, with your heart, and let it speak to you.

The Recluse: How the Isolation Intensified That Part of Me

I'm referencing the child, my inner child, from ages three to six. The biggest influence in my life was my brother Irving. As I alluded to earlier, Irving was different. He had Down Syndrome, with epilepsy, and other genetic anomalies, that I am not sure about. I was not told about them, and only know what my sister may have heard from my parents. She was older and was able to understand what I couldn't. There was one anomaly that created the distance my parents imposed. It seems that he had a tendency toward violent behavior. What I learned from that, was there can be love from a distance, without touch.

What that model did for me was to create a framework for how love is expressed. As mentioned earlier, the isolation simply reinforced that behavior, causing me to feel even more distant from the rest of my world: my neighborhood, my city, and my building: even neighbors so close by. As I sit now, hearing my channel dictate this section of the book, I know all that I write here is truth. There is no reason for anything else.

Having dabbled in the outside world, knowing that everything is my creation, I can change that creation if I so choose. The outside world may change moment to moment, but I am sovereign over this inside world. It can change one last time knowing my truth as it is now. It doesn't have to change if what I have created is love. Love is the greatest truth there is and the greatest emotion the heart and soul can express. Once that expression is fluid, there is nothing else to express. Love is all there is!

This recluse is ready to step into that world of her creation and find others who vibrate in that same way. Life has changed dramatically, yet not at all. It has just revealed itself to me, so I can return to the world as I am now, with whatever reception awaits me.

Sunday

I remember a play that Billy Crystal wrote. It was a one-man show about Sundays. It was a book first, referencing the 700 Sundays he spent with his father before he died. Sundays hold a special significance for me as well. Our family went to visit with my brother on Sundays for the length of time he was at Willowbrook. It was a very dark place, and it was difficult to see him there.

Each Sunday at the end of our visit, I would look back at him sitting on the bench waiting for one of the workers to escort him through that locked door. Each time I wanted to just be with him, for I felt his loneliness, I knew my parents wouldn't allow it, so I never did. After he passed, Sundays were very sad, some worse than others. Here I am at age 72, and Sunday still has that bittersweet edge to it. I would guess that Billy Crystal still feels the same way about his father who passed away when he was a teenager.

The Children

My heart goes out to all the children who are going through this time in Gaia's evolution. Especially the children under age 6, who haven't fully developed emotionally, psychologically, and socially. They are forced into a situation, not of their making, and that part that hasn't quite developed. He or she must wear a mask and wonder what's next with their connection to their families and their friends. Some of these children are getting very sick, for they are too young to be vaccinated.

My own connection to these children has changed. Part of me wants to keep very separate from them. Yet there is so much compassion for them, especially that part of me that is the teacher. There is an irretrievable piece of each of them that will need to be addressed after this pandemic is over, and we all find that "new normal." As I sit here, wondering about the children, it is roughly two weeks until school starts. I will be sending much more love than I have, to support schools here in NY, and all over the country. It is such a vulnerable time!

Back to School

As a former teacher, I watch the long lines of people waiting outside the Board of Education building, which is very close to my house. I wonder how much is about the need for a job, versus people with a true desire to teach in a mighty different way. My guess is their requirements have become very loose for new teachers. I must go back to the understanding that we are all where we need to be, doing what we agreed to do.

Let the games begin, everyone! We are entering a "black hole" with how everyone adjusts to whatever mandates have been agreed upon between the mayor and governor of New York. Knowing the number of schools that are very old, I wonder how prepared those schools are for proper ventilation, and distancing. The opening of schools follows Labor Day weekend, where people may have been lax with how they mingle with friends and family.

As one who isolated a lengthy time, my concern is how the numbers may change following both. My focus this week is about infusing love into this book, as well as the ethers, for everyone's health and safety.

Division

While isolating, the news was filling the airwaves concerning all the groups that have created division in this country, as well as the world. The insurrection on the White House was just the tip of the iceberg. There have been anti-American groups that were literally asleep for decades. Once this insurrection happened, and while it was happening, these groups participated in the activity, hence were noticed for their potential danger to the country. The war of the parties was worse than ever, and we faced months of claims that the election was "stolen." There seemed to be no time to rest, for the news was becoming a nuisance with their views. I had a choice, and I exercised that choice to shut off the TV. I listened to a minimum of information I felt I needed to know, and then it was either writing, a Zoom class, or watching a movie.

What I have learned is how much misinformation has been circulated, along with all the conspiracy theories, and those that won't vaccinate, for they feel there is a "chip" involved. This pandemic won't end either medically or politically until the "forces of good" step up and raise the vibration. The planet needs love, WE need love, I certainly need love. Where is the love--(wasn't that a song?) Politics and misinformation have delayed any lasting peace and healing. It takes many of us writing books to get them out as soon as possible. It is not profit driven, rather it is driven by the desire to make a difference with those on the brink of making better choices.

The Power of Prayer

I have learned, especially during the isolation, how important prayer became for me. Not a religion-based prayer, just prayer to source. As I prayed, I felt that the energy it was producing emanated out not just to neighbors in this building, but to the neighborhood, and the city. Some days I directed the energy to travel even further to the country, and the world. I was not sitting dormant in wait: I was doing something constructive that was helping others.

As I ventured out following the isolation, I was able to focus more on those who needed a little bit more love. What was astounding to me, was how quickly what I sent came back.

Recently, I found that a family member I had been estranged from, needed help with her dog. The dog is almost ready to transition, and that was causing much sadness. I did not consider that we were estranged: rather I responded with sending Love and Light and asking for those in my constructed family group to do the same.

My body had a pronounced response to any attachment, and I knew that it was just what it was: praying for someone who asked for prayers.

Attachment could be a book all by itself. Suffice it to say, when I pray for people, places, or things, it is vital to then let it go. The power of prayer, hence love, has its own direction, and doesn't need me.

Detachment

Practice, practice, practice: if that can get you to Carnegie Hall, then it can also liberate you from toxic thoughts, fear, and trust issues with information we receive from the media, doctors, and simply from the airwaves. I just got home from one of those days where people were too close, unmasked, and the energy was simply too dark. I was guided to write about it, for many feel this way who are in a big city at the end of the summer.

So, the question is: how do you love while sifting through the energy muck that exists? I know the answer for me is: come from a place of love. Love can move mountains, right? Okay move this place called Brooklyn Heights into a loving environment, where people are smiling through their masks! Working on it!

The Party's Over

It's time to call it a day... This book needs to be shared, now! This time that we are all experiencing has no end date. But this book does! The Clarion Calls: what is that you ask? It's the title of my next song, channeled by the Archangel Metatron. He guided me to put a package down on the piano keys last week. It hit all the black keys, and I had to figure out the sequence of the notes. There is one white note to end what sounds like a call to action. It is!

We are all called into action to spread love and heal the planet. How? Love yourself first (like a mother to a child), and then send that love out to the world. Gaia needs it: she'll feel it and use it to heal this Mother Earth. One person I spoke with today said: "But it's too late, the damage is done." I said, "No it isn't!" I assured him that love has already won. Earth will survive this huge shift in consciousness and vibration. We just need to stick to the plan: spread love!

Acknowledgments

I would like to acknowledge the following people for their support with the writing of this book : Hans Christian King for suggesting from Source that there was a book I needed to write, Owl Willows for helping me to convert from being a composer to being a writer as well, Christian who singularly represents thousands of students over 25 years who I have had the same impact with. Gerri for reminding me how very beautiful my writing is as I read it to her, to the people in my group with John Burgos: Eileen, Tara, Judy, Alyssa, Shary Lou, and many others in the LITE Group, Archangel Michael, Gabriel, Jeshua. To Meg, for suggesting the piano as a way of seeing two sides.

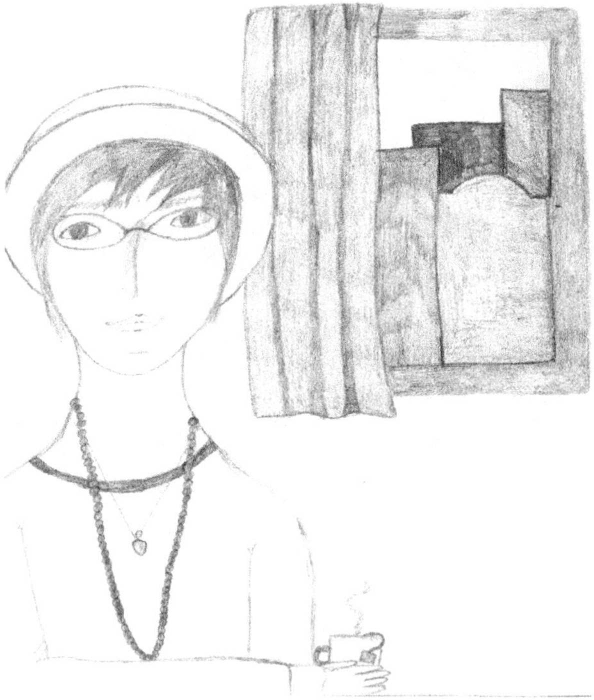

About

Since the lockdown in March of 2020, who I am has changed. In my heart of hearts, who I am is more of a mystery to me. I have learned that the only moment that matters is this one. I suppose I've always known that, but it became more pronounced as I sat in isolation. I was able, in the silence, to delve deeper into who I want to present to the world, both inner and out. The music flowed from that discovery and kept flowing until that "well" dried up enough to allow this book to be expressed. What the book did was to merge all the identities I once was, with who I experience as the Ilene that is emerging. She is kind, loving, honest, creative, sometimes melancholy, and always there for those in need. This book ends a chapter for me, to enable another one that may include an account of this new life. Stay tuned…